THE POWER
of
LETTING GO

Rev. J Martin

DEDICATION

I dedicate this book to my mother, who always
believed I would do great things with my life. .

CONTENTS

ACKNOWLEDGMENTS

I would like to thank everyone who made this book possible. To all that support me, and continue to support me, which includes YOU.

1 Power Of Letting Go

We all have a tendency to hold onto things. Maybe a person hurt you in the past, and you can't forget about it. Maybe you had a fallout with a neighbor and no longer speak. You put your heart into a relationship, only for it to be broken. You worked hard for a promotion, but failed to get it.

One of the best things you can do is release it and let it go. If you let the thoughts replay in your mind, going over and over what was said or done, questioning yourself what you could have done differently or why God didn't answer your prayers, all that will do is lead to anger, pain, and frustration. When those feelings build up, it can cause worry and sickness.

It may not feel fair to you, as it may be something that hurt you or a family member greatly, but if you can learn to release it, it is an act of faith. You are saying, God, I trust in your better judgment. You said all things are for my greater good; maybe what happened is a test of how strong my character is.

There is great power in letting go. Don't let go of your dreams or your promises. Let go of the stress and frustration you feel when things don't go your way. Take your hands off the wheel, jump into the passenger's seat, and let God take control. God can see the best path for your life. Learn to say; God I will let you take me where you want me to go. This is the best way to live.

Often, we will trust God and be strong in our faith if God does it our way. When it's going smoothly, God is our best friend, but when things don't, we question if God is listening. Truth is, maybe what you want is not in line with what God knows is best for you..

2 I Will Catch You

There was this cleaner on the side of a building and the pulley snapped, he slipped, but just when he thought all was lost, he reached out a hand and caught the bar on the underside of the platform. He just couldn't reach his other hand up to get a firm grip. He cried out to the heavens, is anybody up there?

To his surprise a voice said, Yes, son what do you need.

He said, "God, I can't hold on any longer, please rescue me."

God said, "ok son, let go of the platform and I will catch you."

After a long pause, the man said, "Is there anyone else up there?"

That's the way we act a lot of the time, God I need your help but I want you to do it my way. The way I have planned, the way I want. In order for God to help us, we have to be willing to let go.

Maybe someone in your life didn't live up to your expectations, they said something that rubbed you up the wrong way, or hurts you. Instead of being frustrated, step back and look at the bigger picture; maybe God is giving you a message, that person is not who you thought they were. Maybe God closed the door because it leads to a dead end; he has something better lined up if you would only open up to him.

We all like to be in control of our lives, but sometimes it's better if we sit in the passenger seat and let God take over. He will bring you to the people and situations that are the best for you.

3 New House

A friend was looking for a new house. He had done well for himself and wanted to start his family with a nice home, with the things he didn't have as a child, so he could bring up his children with all that he wished for.

After months of looking, he found a lovely place. It had a lovely garden at the front and a large, flat garden at the back, perfect for playing football. It also had a garage, with an adjoining swimming pool.

They made a very strong offer, just under the asking price, as it had been on the market for some time, and they were sure it would be theirs. After making the offer, they waited and heard no reply. It was the first house they had tried to buy and were unsure of the process.

No one lived in the house, so in the evening, they would visit the house and make plans on what they would do. They asked me to pray that all would go through with no problems.

Three weeks later, they got a call from the real estate people, saying sorry, but the owner had sold to someone else. They were very disappointed, as they believed, and prayed, and stood in faith.

Scripture says that God's ways are not our ways. They are higher and better than our ways. Sometimes, what we are praying for is not what God has in store for us. We have good intentions, but God loves us too much to answer that prayer.

I have found that anything you need to be happy will often lead you to be out of balance. If you need to have that house, that car, that job to be happy, then you are putting too much focus on it. If you don't get it, it can lead to unhappiness, feelings of lack, feelings that God is not listening, even a test of your faith.

Be mature enough to hand that dream to him. Pray to him, saying, God, I want this; this is what I would like to happen; this is what would bring me happiness, but you know what is best for me, and if it doesn't happen my way, on my timetable, then I will not get upset or bitter or have feelings of frustration. God, I trust you. My life is in your hands.

At first, my friends felt discouraged, as if God had let them down. I didn't see or hear from them for many weeks. Eventually, they contacted me and said the wind had been taken out of their sails. They were deflated. Then, they shared how their faith had been restored, and they let it go. They said God knows best for us.

About a month later, they came across an older, run down home in a nice neighborhood close to the city, where both worked; plus, it was less than a mile away from the local primary school. They bought the house and renovating it to its former glory, building an extension to include a swimming pool, all for less than the previous house.

My friend and his wife came to me, saying, it was as if the moment they let go of the disappointment of not getting the other house, God brought them to the perfect house.

One of my main prayers I shared with them and will now share with you is, God, not my will, but may your will be done. If a door closes, it is not the end of the world or need for frustration or worry. Learn to let it go.

If my plans don't work out or someone does something against me, it's no big deal. I have learned to let it go and hand it over to God. There are better things in store for me.

.

4 Directing Our Steps

Proverbs 20:24
Since God is directing our steps, why try to figure out everything that happens along the way?

Many of you have probably gone through disappointments. It didn't seem fair. You didn't understand it. You did your best, but someone let you down. It can easily lead to bitterness and frustration or you to give up on your dreams.

It's important to remember that God is in your life, right now. He is directing your steps. What you think is a setback often turns out to be for the best. If you are open to it and not caught up in the past, you will find that God is getting you into position to take you to a new level.

Get into agreement with God, shake off the self-pity, and shake off the disappointment. Stop thinking that God has let you down, that he hasn't answered your prayers. No, God is directing you every step of the way. That disappointment may not have seemed fair, but it is all part of your destiny.

If you will let it go and move forward, then you will come into something greater that God has in store for you. Better friends, a better job, and a deeper faith.

5 Artistic Touch

A good friend of my brother is an excellent artist and was slowly getting noticed by the right people. Then, his father became sick. I prayed with the family. We believed he would get better and stood in faith. Unfortunately, his father went to be with the Lord. Our prayers were not answered the way we wanted.

He took it hard, as he would go everywhere with his father. They were more like brothers than father and son. If you needed to find them on a Saturday, everyone knew they would be in the pub, watching football or rugby.

When we pray for something that we really want and it doesn't work out, it's easy to get discouraged, to get bitter. My brother's friend was very discouraged; he had lost his best friend. He stopped doing art shows and then stopped doing art altogether. He came to me almost a year later and told me he had to get an office job, as he gave up on his art. He couldn't even focus on his stressful office job and was thinking of giving it up, too.

I knew his father well. I knew his loss was still playing on his mind. I said to him, would your father want you to be living his way? He replied, of course not. He would be very disappointed if he knew I gave up my art. I could see his eyes light up. Then I said to him, "Although your father may not be here, physically, he will still be looking down on you and want you to make him proud."

Within 6 months, he had a new exhibition at a local gallery. He had put his heart and soul into every painting. You could see the raw emotion in each piece. His exhibition got spotted by a Dublin businessman, who asked him to do an exhibition in Dublin that got him recognized as one of Ireland's up and coming Artists.

Sure, there is a proper time for mourning, but you cannot let a season of mourning turn into a lifetime of mourning. At some point, you have to say, "God I'm letting it go. Yes, I'm disappointed; yes, it's hard, but just because my loved one has died doesn't mean your plan for my life has ended."

When you go through the loss of a family member or a relationship of any kind, it can be difficult. Many people can let it get to them. They become depressed, negative, bitter, or all three. It can be hard, but if you can let it go, saying, God I don't understand why you put this in my path, but I trust you. You are still in control. Then you will step into the next level of your destiny.

I have learned in my life that God doesn't always take you on a direct path. There will be many detours. It's better if you don't try to figure it out, but simply learn to trust in him.

6 Why?

I get questioned a lot; Reverend, why did I not get the promotion? Why did I get laid off at work? Why did my marriage not work out?

Here's my answer. I don't know why. You may never know why. What I know is God is directing your steps. It may not seem fair, but God is fair. Sometimes, it may seem like a setback, but you will see, eventually, God will repay you for the unfair thing that happened.

If you could learn to let go of some of the things you are holding onto, you will find you will come into breakthroughs, to promotions, to peace of mind. As long as you are holding onto the old, you can never experience the new.

Many people have come to me over the last few years, asking, why did I lose my house or my savings and my neighbor didn't? My answer is always the same. I don't know.

Isaiah 61:3
"To bestow on them a crown of beauty instead of ashes, the oil of joy instead of mourning, and a garment of praise instead of a spirit of despair."

It's up to you to let go of the ashes, let go of the mourning, let go of the spirit of despair. Let go of the hurts and pains. Stop trying to work out why something bad has happened to you, because that will only lead to frustration.

There are situations we face to which there are no logical explanations. It's a test of your character. You have to say; I don't know why this has happened, and I'm ok with that.

You are God, and I am not. Your ways are better than my ways. Since you are controlling my every step, I will not waste the time or energy trying to work out everything that happens along the way. It's a powerful way to live and a way that is worth striving for.

Most of the time, we can deal with a situation if we can explain it in our minds. This happened for this reason. He got into trouble, because he hangs around with the wrong people. She lost her job, because she was the last into the company. My neighbors went bankrupt, because they were always buying and buying.

The thing is, sometimes, things don't make sense. It doesn't make sense for my brother to work in a job for 20 years and get laid off. It doesn't make sense for an innocent child to get knocked down by a drunk driver.

What do we do when something happens that we can't explain?

We have to learn to let it go, pass it over to God. If you try to work out why you didn't get the promotion, why your son didn't get the grades, then it will lead to frustration, anger, and bitterness.

If God wants you to know why, then he will tell you, but if he doesn't, then you need to learn to LET IT GO and walk away. Initially, it will be hard, as our brains are programmed to find the reason, but often, the reason can be 3 years up the road.

Proverbs 25:2
It is the glory of God to conceal a matter.

If you will trust in God, then accept that there will be unanswered prayers. We are not meant to understand every path that God will take us down. He, and only he, knows the way.

One thing I know from experience is: God is loving, God is fair, and God does not take something away, unless he puts something better in its place.

Here's what I have learned. Don't knock on a door that God has closed. If you stood in faith, prayed, and believed, and it didn't work out, then God closed that door. So move forward.

When my brother's friend's father was sick, I prayed with his family, but his father went to be with the Lord. God closed that chapter of their lives. His son questioned God's decision for over a year, but when he accepted God's decision, his life blossomed.

Don't question the things that seemingly go against you. If you applied for a new job and didn't get it, it wasn't the right job for you. Learn to LET IT GO. God has something better lined up.

7 When God Closes A Door

A young man came to see me recently. He was engaged, and the girl broke it off 3 months before the wedding. She had been seeing someone else. 6 months later, he was still in deep depression and had lost his job. I told him what I'm telling you.

God can close a door to save you from even deeper heartache.

Don't question his decision, thinking you were at fault, getting into depression. Stand up tall and realize that chapter is over, and it's time to turn the page. LET IT GO.

3 months later, he returned to thank me for the advice. He told me he had started to socialize again and met a lovely girl, who was careful with her money and didn't drink to excess, like his previous girlfriend.

When you move forward, you will come into another chapter. The good news is; your story doesn't end in defeat. It ends in victory. God always has something better in store for you. When obstacles are put in your path, sometimes, it can be for you to learn, to expand, and to evolve as a person. Maybe the person you think is perfect for you is actually harmful, but your love blinds you from seeing it.

Proverbs 3:5-6
Trust in the Lord with all your heart, and do not lean on your own understanding. In all your ways acknowledge him, and he will make straight your paths.

Maybe you have done everything possible. You stood in faith, you prayed, and you attended service. You went without as an offering, but things didn't work out. The best thing you can do is release it and LET IT GO.

8 Be Like David

Be like David in 2 Samuel 12. When his baby was sick, he fasted and prayed that God would take pity on him and let his baby live. When the news came to him that the baby had died, his servants were surprised that he washed and ate, and they asked him why? To which he replied. "Now that the baby is dead, why should I fast? I can't bring him back to life. Someday, I will go to him, but he cannot come back to me."

If things don't work out, do like David. Accept that it is out of your control and move on, understanding that God has something better in store for you. In David's case, God graced him with another child, Solomon.

If he had spent time in pity and bitterness that God had taken away his child, David and his wife may not have even tried for another child. Take David's lesson and get ready for the new thing that God will put into your life.

When you go through things you don't understand, it is not the end. It's a new beginning. You will find that, if you can learn to release it and let it go, God will deliver something better in its place. You will gain more in the future than you have lost in the past.

The next time you get into your car, notice the size of the front windscreen, compared to the size of the rear view mirror. This is because what is up ahead is more important than what you have already passed. Where you are going is far more important than where you have been.

If you let your thoughts dwell in the past, then you will get stuck in the past, and when looking back, you cannot see where you are going and can easily lose your way. Don't let one setback ruin your life. Don't let losing that job, that relationship, that house define who you are. Each step on the journey is simply another step on the road to your divine destiny.

Learn to LET IT GO and prepare for the new thing God has in store.

Stop focusing on something you cannot change. If God closed a door, don't try to reopen it or work out why he closed it with worry or pity. Instead, look for the other door he has opened for you. He has another job, another relationship, and more new friends lined up.

Psalms 131 1-2

"I do not concern myself with matters that are too great for me. But I have calmed and quieted myself, I am like a weaned child with its mother; like a weaned child I am content."

David knew that what happened with his baby was beyond his understanding. Instead of getting angry or bitter, he calmed and quieted himself, and he was content.

When we go through things we don't understand, we must do like David. Learn to be calm and quiet ourselves, and with that will come contentment. Know that God has something better in store, a new chapter better than the last.

Friends, when you can let things go and not become angry or bitter, then the creator of the universe will come into your life and create what can, sometimes, seem like miracles, but you should be open, expecting great things.

9 London Lawyer

An old college friend got a job in London for a leading law firm. He was doing well and moved up through the company quickly. Then, he had a falling out with a partner within the company. A lot of unfair accusations came against him, and he was forced to resign.

His dreams had been shattered and so was his reputation. He was forced to sell his apartment in central London and move home. I spoke to him, and he was deeply depressed and didn't feel like applying for new jobs. Not only was his dream crushed, but so was his spirit.

At a social gathering in his local town, he got into a conversation with a young woman who needed advice, as her father had given her control of his Irish property developments, which had come to a standstill over some red tape. Her father was attending to some business in New York and was tied up for a couple of weeks. She didn't want to contact him, as it would show she wasn't up to the responsibility.

She explained the problem in full, and my friend told her he had plenty of experience in that area and knew the proper people to contact. He said he no longer practiced law, but would get her the correct information, which she could present to her solicitor with the instructions to carry out what was needed.

All went smoothly, and the development was back on track. On her father's return, she told him how much my friend had helped. Her father was very impressed and called my friend to thank him, as his approach saved the company a lot of money.

He met my friend, as he was also having problems with his New York deal. My friend's advice found a loophole his lawyers had overlooked.

Again, very impressed, he offered my friend a job for legal advice that would include dealings overlooking his properties in Dubai, Barcelona, London, and New York.

1 Corinthians 13:12
"Now I know in part; then I shall know fully."

Initially, my friend thought his world had fallen apart. He saw no hope. Years of study and hard work had been thrown in his face. He only knew in part.

His new job gives him freedom he could only have dreamt about in his old job. Now, my friend knows fully. He had to lose, what he thought to be his dream job, to find a job that let him travel all over the world, a job that let him work anywhere with an internet connection.

There might be a lot of things happening in your life that you don't understand, but one day, they will make sense. Now, you only know in part, but one day, you will know in full.

One day, you will look back in amazement and see, like my friend did, even through the toughest times, God is working in your life. At the moment, it may seem like God is not fair, but God is fair.

God can take what may seem like an injustice and bring good out of it. He can take a betrayal and open a greater door. It takes a lot of faith, but learn to trust him. Learn to take your hands off the wheel and let him do the driving.

LET GO of the need to have it your way.

When something happens you don't understand, learn to LET IT GO.

Some of you, today, will have things weighing you down. Learn to LET IT GO. Turn it over to God; he will not let you down. For everything you have lost, God has something better lined up.

If you can learn to let go of that hurt, disappointment, or setback, then you will find, as you let go, God can get to work. I see too many people hold onto things that have happened, sometimes, years ago. It makes them bitter and angry, which blocks them from God's power.

When you learn to LET GO, he will open a new world to you. He will pay you back for any injustice; bring you to stronger and more meaningful relationships. Nothing will stand in your way. You will become everything God created you to be.

10 First Steps

Letting go of old thought patterns can be easier said than done. When I mention this to people, they will often say, yes, in theory, that sounds amazing, but my neighbor really hurt me, and it plays over and over again on the screen of my mind. How can I stop that? How can I let it go?

The problem lies in the fact that we often get lost in our thinking. Thinking is based on either the past or the future. Thinking about the past leads to anger, regret, sadness or grief. Thinking of the future leads to anxiety, fear, worry, and stress.

Many years ago I had a lot of personal problems, the same message kept playing on my mind. Even when I would pray for it, it would be on my mind. There seemed like no escape until I was introduced to the eastern concept of living in the present moment. Mindfulness.

Most Important Lesson

Everybody knows that everything is happening now. Everything else is just past and future. Most people understand this but don't live it. This is why humans are stressed, unhappy and frustrated. They are constantly lost in the past and future.

The mind likes to continually analyze events, trying to work things out, to see patterns, attempting to use the past to predict the future.

My mind kept replaying the same message. If only I had been there more often, a certain thing may not have happened. Looking back, Yes, I might have been right, but events had happened, and my presence was no longer going to be of any use.

I have read several books on mindfulness. What I learned from them is:

God is only in the present moment.

If you are thinking about the past, if only I had done more studying; if only I had spent more time with a loved one; if only I had worked harder I would have got the promotion.

Then you are blocking God love from flowing into your life.

If you are thinking about the future, what if they don't like me? What if I don't say the right thing? What if I don't get the job? What if I get ill and can't repay my car payments.

Then you doubt Gods plan. You are blocking God's love flowing into your life, not trusting in him that all will work out.

What I started out doing on a daily basis was listening to a mindfulness exercise that I have a link to in the kindle edition, that comes free when you buy this book.

Once upon waking and once before bed. In the beginning there may seem no major difference but in time the calmness that these moments bring will flow into your everyday life.

ABOUT THE AUTHOR

I live on the northwest coast of Ireland. I use this medium to share my true voice. I wish to enlighten others and help them to see that God wants the very best for them. We often make it hard for him to enter our lives as we focus on the dark clouds rather than the silver lining.

In this growing digital frontier, I just want to shed a little light out into the world, to light up peoples lives in the hope that they to will help inspire others; which will slowly but surely change the world, even in a small way.

My Other Books

The Power Of Choice

The Power Of Words

God's Perfect Timing

Make Space For God

Made in the USA
San Bernardino, CA
13 July 2020

75389251R10024